Water Therapy

Enriching Mind, Body, and Soul

Bridgitt Bradley-Brown and Dion Lucas

TEACH Services, Inc.
PUBLISHING
www.TEACHServices.com • (800) 367-1844

World rights reserved. This book or any portion thereof may not be copied or reproduced in any form or manner whatever, except as provided by law, without the written permission of the publisher, except by a reviewer who may quote brief passages in a review.

The author assumes full responsibility for the accuracy of all facts and quotations as cited in this book. The opinions expressed in this book are the author's personal views and interpretations, and do not necessarily reflect those of the publisher.

This book is provided with the understanding that the publisher is not engaged in giving spiritual, legal, medical, or other professional advice. If authoritative advice is needed, the reader should seek the counsel of a competent professional.

Copyright © 2019 Bridgitt Bradley-Brown and Dion Lucas

Copyright © 2019 TEACH Services, Inc.

ISBN-13: 978-1-4796-1024-2 (Paperback)

ISBN-13: 978-1-4796-1025-9 (ePub)

Scripture references labeled (KJV) are taken from the King James Version of the Bible. Public domain.

Scripture references labeled (NIV) are taken from the Holy Bible, New International Version®, NIV® Copyright ©1973, 1978, 1984, 2011 by Biblica, Inc.® Used by permission. All rights reserved worldwide.

Preface

Bridgitt Bradley-Brown and Dion Lucas attend First Missionary Baptist Church in Huntsville, Alabama, and they were attending a vacation bible school (VBS) class in the summer of 2018 that sparked this water therapy book. Bridgitt was instructing a women's VBS class to answer this question. "What would you do differently in your past life?" Dion responded by saying, "I would drink more water!"

Drinking plenty of water can help a person eat less foods, prevent dehydration, and improve skin complexion. However, a person should also thirst for spiritual water because there is great comfort in God's holy words from the Bible. Enjoy this new wellness book to enrich your mind, body, and soul.

Table of Content

- **W**ord of God
- **A**bstaining
- **T**herapy
- **E**nrichment
- **R**est

Word of God

The **W** in "**W**ATER" represents the Word of God. In the creation story of the Jewish Torah and Christian Bible, God's spirit first moved "over the face of the waters" and God said, "Let the waters bring forth swarms of living creatures" (Genesis 1:2, 20). In Islam, water is the origin of all life on Earth. The Qur'an says water is the substance from which God created the human being (25:54) and even says that at creation, God's throne "was upon water" (11:7). If you think about the fact that our bodies are made up of 75% (or more) of water, just imagine what these simple things can do to our physiology!

Abstaining

The **A** in "**WA**TER" represents abstaining. Abstaining means that a person is disciplined in their actions, which is one of the fruits of the Spirit, or having self-control (Galatians 5: 22–23). Practicing self-control comes from establishing healthy habits. Researchers have suggested that it takes a minimum of twenty-one days to make something a habit. If a person is not accustomed to drinking eight glasses of water a day, then we recommend starting out with four glasses of water. You can drink a glass before breakfast, during your breaks, at lunch, and during dinner time. Then, gradually increase your intake each week until it becomes an active component of your daily diet.

Therapy

The **T** in "**WA T ER**" represents therapy. For decades, it has been a well-known habit in Japan to drink water immediately after waking up every morning (on an empty stomach). This is referred to as Japanese water therapy. This habit is highly recommended because of its natural health benefits.

Japanese water therapy helps relieve stress, promotes weight loss, and ensures a strong digestive system. Most of all, it keeps you energetic throughout the day. Drinking enough water during the day also revs up your metabolism. Ayurveda experts also suggest that you must drink water first thing in the morning as it plays a key role in boosting your overall health.

Ayurvedic medicine ("Ayurveda" for short) is one of the world's oldest holistic ("whole-body") healing systems. It was developed more than 3,000 years ago in India. It's based on the belief that health and wellness depend on a delicate balance between the mind, body, and spirit. Its main goal is to promote good health, not fight disease. But treatments may be geared toward specific health problems. In the United States, it's considered a form of complementary and alternative medicine.

Water is an essential part of our lives and it is one of the basic elements required for human survival. It is often advised that one must drink at least eight to ten glasses of water every day to flush out all the toxins and to help the body function properly. In similar fashion to the Ayurveda experts, some nutritionists also advise that is great to start you day with a glass of water on an empty stomach. It kick-starts your metabolism and does wonders for your overall health. In fact, people in Japan take this advice quite seriously and practice a certain kind of water therapy that is known to help with weight loss and fitness. A simple practice when done methodically and consistently may help in fighting various health problems. The objective of this therapy is to use water in your daily life to balance and regulate your health.

Water Therapy

Scientists also believe that being by large bodies of water can be beneficial. Just think—going to the beach can reduce stress, increase your creativity, and reduce feelings of depression! Water is one of mother nature's cure-alls. Water is full of naturally occurring elements and minerals that can help you feel at ease. So, whether you're jumping into a pool or dipping your toes in the ocean, you're definitely going to experience a feeling of relaxation. Water can be a great way to quickly boost your mood! Being in "blue space" can help you clear your head and approach your problems in a more creative manner. Similar to meditation, the beach can ignite a feeling of stillness that allows you to shut out everything else and focus on something positive.

Salt Water Therapy

Another form of water therapy is sensory deprivation flotation. It is essentially a giant enclosed bathtub or tank filled with salt and water used for restricted environmental stimulation therapy (or REST—aptly named!). The abundance of salt makes your body float. When you let go of tension—whether physically, emotionally, or mentally—you feel lighter. Both the mind and the body can release and unfold through the support of water therapy in a way that no other therapy can replicate.

Therapies Continued ...

Hot and cold plunges are helpful resources to recover the body from aches and pains. You would think something as simple as alternating hot and cold baths or showers couldn't possibly make that much of a change in your body. Think again. It has been shown to increase circulation, speed healing, promote lymphatic drainage, and boost the immune system.

Get your steam on! Steaming is an important part of cleansing the body. Our skin is the largest organ of detoxification, so sweating out toxins can release impurities and make us feel clear and rejuvenated.

Take a dip in the ocean ... or any natural body of water. If you don't want to take the dive, even getting your feet wet in salt water draws out toxins and gives you the benefits of marinating in the healing negative ions that are said to release serotonin, alleviate depression, relieve stress, and increase energy.

Enrichment

The **E** in "**WATER**" represent enrichment. The following enriching scriptures are provided to reference spiritual effects of water to enhance your mind, body, and soul. May these scriptures encourage you to thirst after God's word and heal you from the inside out.

Water Therapy Cleanses the Body

"Wash and make yourselves clean. Take your evil deeds out of my sight; stop doing wrong" (Isaiah 1: 16, NIV).

Water Therapy Decreases Headaches

Physical and spiritual water is key to overcoming battlefields of the mind. *"Trust in the Lord with all thine heart; and lean not unto thine own understanding. In all thy ways acknowledge him, and he shall direct thy paths"* (Proverbs 3: 5, 6, KJV).

Water Therapy Prevents Dehydration

To the Woman at the Well,

"Jesus answered, 'Everyone who drinks this water will be thirsty again, but whoever drinks the water I give them will never thirst. Indeed, the water I give them will become in them a spring of water welling up to eternal life'" (John 4:13, 14, NIV).

Water Therapy Eases Constipation

Let Go and Let God! *"Then the word of the Lord came to Jeremiah: 'I am the Lord, the God of all mankind. Is anything too hard for me?'"* (Jeremiah 32:26, 27, NIV).

Water Therapy Loosens Joints

Water aerobics are a good source of exercise. *"Do you not know that your bodies are temples of the Holy Spirit, who is in you, whom you have received from God? You are not your own; you were bought at a price. Therefore, honor God with your bodies"* (1 Corinthians 6: 19, 20, NIV).

Water Therapy Allows the Body to Eat Less

Hydrate with water to consume less foods because people tend to eat more when they are dehydrated. Physical and spiritual water are equally important. *"Jesus answered, 'It is written: "Man shall not live on bread alone, but on every word that comes from the mouth of God"'"* (Mathew 4:4, NIV).

Water Therapy Helps the Complexion

You can have and inner and outer glow with Christ. *"Jesus answered, 'You are the light of the world. A town built on a hill cannot be hidden. Neither do people light a lamp and put it under a bowl. Instead they put it on its stand, and it gives light to everyone in the house. In the same way, let your light shine before others, that they may see your good deeds and glorify your Father in heaven'"* (Matthew 5:14, 16, NIV).

R.I.C.E.

It wasn't until Bridgitt and Dion played competitive sports that they discovered how helpful and essential water is to personal wellbeing! As former athletes, they used the RICE Method for healing personal injuries. The first step to recovery is to rest! If you've ever hurt your ankle or had another type of sprain or strain, chances are your doctor recommended **REST** followed by **ICING** the injury, **COMPRESSING** it, and provide proper **ELEVATION**. The RICE method is a simple self-care technique that helps reduce swelling, ease pain, and speed up healing. You can treat minor injuries with the RICE method at home. You might try it if you have an achy knee, ankle, or wrist after playing sports. If you have pain or swelling that gets worse or doesn't go away, see a doctor.

Sabbath Rest

The **R** in **"WATER"** represents rest. One of the fundamental principles of the Bible when it comes to time management is the Sabbath. According to the Bible, it is about more than just taking time off. After creating the world, God looked around and saw that *"it was very good"* (Genesis 1:31). God did not just cease from His labor; he stopped and enjoyed what He had made. What does this mean for us? We need to stop to enjoy God, to enjoy His creation, to enjoy the fruits of our labor. The whole point of Sabbath is joy in what God has done. In the Bible, Sabbath rest means to cease regularly from and to enjoy the results of your work. It provides balance: *"Six days you shall labor and do all your work, but the seventh day is a sabbath to the Lord your God"* (Exodus 20:9, 10). Although Sabbath rest receives a much smaller amount of time than work, it is a necessary counterbalance so that the rest of your work can be good and beneficial.

We invite you to view the complete
selection of titles we publish at:
www.TEACHServices.com

We encourage you to write us
with your thoughts about this,
or any other book we publish at:
info@TEACHServices.com

TEACH Services' titles may be purchased in
bulk quantities for educational, fund-raising,
business, or promotional use.
bulksales@TEACHServices.com

Finally, if you are interested in seeing
your own book in print, please contact us at:
publishing@TEACHServices.com

We are happy to review your manuscript at no charge.

www.ingramcontent.com/pod-product-compliance
Lightning Source LLC
Chambersburg PA
CBHW061119170426
43200CB00023B/2997